D1106270

to teachers and parents

This is a LADYBIRD LEADER book, one of a series specially produced to meet the very real need for carefully planned *first information books* that instantly attract enquiring minds and stimulate reluctant readers.

The subject matter and vocabulary have been selected with expert assistance, and the brief and simple text is printed in large, clear type.

Children's questions are anticipated and facts presented in a logical sequence. Where possible, the books show what happened in the past and what is relevant today.

Special artwork has been commissioned to set a standard rarely seen in books for this reading age and at this price.

Full colour illustrations are on all 48 pages to give maximum impact and provide the extra enrichment that is the aim of all Ladybird Leaders.

Acknowledgment
The photograph on pages 40-41
is by courtesy of Ranks Hovis McDougall Ltd.

A Ladybird Leader

bread

by P. B. Roscoe

with illustrations by
Jennifer Moore and Gerald Witcomb
and photographs by John Moyes

Ladybird Books Ltd Loughborough 1977

Early bread

The first bread was made about 8,000 years ago.

It must have tasted very different from the bread we eat today.

Nowadays bread supplies us
with nearly a quarter
of the nourishment we need
to keep us healthy.

The raw material of bread

Flour is used to make bread.
It is made from *cereal* plants.
There are many different kinds
of cereal, and they are all
members of the grass family.

Oats

Wheat

Maize

Barley

Another source of flour

Long ago some Red Indians
made flour from acorns.

The bread they made from this
tasted bitter
and never became popular.

Wheat

Most of the flour we use today
comes from a cereal called wheat.

When it is fully grown
'ears' of grain appear
at the top of the stem.

A grain of wheat
has three main parts:
the husk, the white filling
and the wheat germ.

White flour is made
from the white filling.

husk

white
filling

wheat
germ

What makes bread rise?

Yeast is a kind of fungus
which is added to the bread
to make it rise.

You can do a simple experiment
to show this.

Put a small amount of yeast
into a bowl.

Add a teaspoonful of sugar
and a little warm water.

Put the bowl in a warm place
for about 10 minutes.
You will then see
that the yeast has grown.
This is called *fermentation*.

How bread is made

Flour is mixed with yeast and water
to form a soft dough.

The dough is then put
in a warm place to rise *(proving)*.

During this time the dough expands
to twice its original size.

This is called *risen* dough.

The risen dough is then baked
at high temperature in an oven.

After this the bread is ready
to eat.

There is a recipe for making bread
on pages 46-49.

The first bread

In prehistoric times
men ate the seeds of grasses.

Perhaps some of the seeds
were hard to crack
with their teeth.

They probably pounded the seeds
between two stones
and produced flour.

They found that
the flour tasted better
if a little water was added.

Cooking the mixture on a hot stone
further improved the flavour.

This was the first bread.

The bread of ancient Egypt

The ancient Egyptians grew
vast fields of wheat.

When the wheat was full grown
the king would cut the first sheaf
with a golden sickle.

This was the signal
for the harvest to begin.

The Egyptians were the first people
to add yeast to their bread.
The yeast made the bread rise.
It was then called *leavened* bread.

Roman bakers

The early Romans were
the first people to have bakers' shops.

Many different grades of bread
were sold.

If you were poor you would buy
the coarse, heavy, dark bread.

The finer white bread
was more expensive.

Each loaf was stamped
with the baker's name.

One bakery, owned by two brothers,
produced 150,000 loaves every day.

Early bread in Britain

Two thousand years ago in Britain most of the people were eating barley bread.

But as time went on rye bread called *maslin* became more popular.

A Roman mill

In Roman times donkeys were used to work the flour mills.

These donkeys had only one rest day every year.

Water mills

It was the Romans who found
another source of power
for grinding corn.

This was called the water mill.

These mills could run
day and night
and grind a vast amount of corn.

In the year 1086
there were 7,500 water mills
at work in Britain.

23

Windmills

At the end of the 12th century
new machines were built
to help the miller.

These were called windmills.

They used
the power of the wind
instead of water.

By the year 1815
there were 10,000 windmills
working in England.

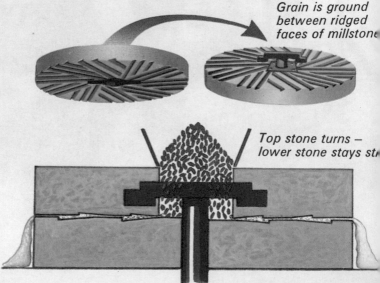

Grain is ground
between ridged
faces of millstone

Top stone turns –
lower stone stays st

The 'Assize of Bread'

In the Middle Ages
any sudden increase
in the price of a loaf
often led to riots and rebellion.

Because of this the government
introduced a law
called the 'Assize of Bread'.

This law fixed
the price of a loaf at one penny
but also allowed the baker
to make a fair profit.

Any baker who broke this law
was tied to a hurdle
and dragged through the streets.

A loaf of his bread
was tied around his neck.

The trend to white bread

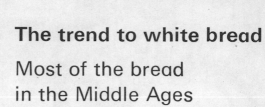

Most of the bread
in the Middle Ages
was dark brown or black,
and it was coarse
and hard to chew.

It was called
'Poor man's bread'
because only rich people
could afford
the finer white bread.

As time went on
more and more people wanted
white bread.

By the 17th century
everyone could buy it,
and even prisoners were given it.

No one knew that brown bread
had more goodness in it.

The early harvests

Because so much bread was needed the harvest was very important.

The wheat was cut, tied in sheaves and then left to dry in the sun.

When it was dry, the grains of wheat were beaten from the stalks.

This was called threshing.

If the harvest was a good one,
there would be a great celebration.

Harvest Festivals
are still held today.

The public bakers

In this country public bakers
have existed for hundreds of years.

As early as 1100
London had two public bakers.

It was not until the 19th century
that they became more common.

People had discovered
it was easier
to buy their bread
than bake it themselves.

Making whiter bread

White bread became so popular
that bakers started to add things
to make it whiter.

Chalk was often used,
and also chemicals
such as white lead and alum.

These *additives* were sometimes
highly poisonous.

Today chemicals are added to bread
to make it easier to bake,
keep longer, and taste better.

Every chemical that is used
is specially tested
to make sure it is harmless.

Roller milling

In the early 1900s
a new process called *roller milling*
was invented.

This method of milling
made it easier to separate the flour
from the husks and wheat germ.

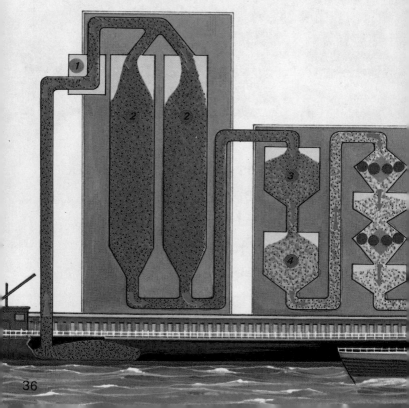

It also made flour cheaper to produce.

KEY

1   Wheat is drawn up by elevator and weighed
2   Silo bins for storing grain
3   Washing wheat (screen room)
4   Drying and conditioning
5   Wheat grain is broken between rollers
6   Sifting
7   Wheat is further broken down
8   Second sifting
9   Purifier
10 Particles are crushed into flour
11 Final sifting
12 Flour is stored in silo bins
13 Bulk flour transporter

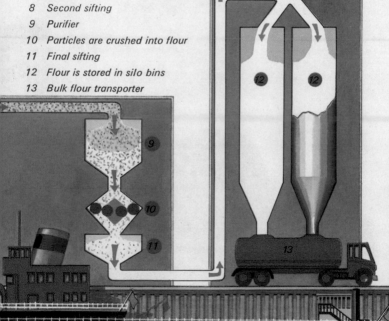

Combine harvesters

So much wheat is needed today
that complicated machines are used
to harvest it.

These machines are called
combine harvesters.

They do all the work
of cutting and threshing
in one operation.

The corn is held against the cutting knife by the sail.
It is then carried on a conveyor belt to a series of
drums and sieves which beat the grain from the 'ears'
of corn and sift out the chaff. The waste straw is
thrown out behind the machine, while the corn is
either stored in a large tank or delivered direct
into a trailer alongside.

Modern flour mills

Modern flour mills rely
almost completely on machines.
The miller has to keep watch
on hundreds of dials and switches.

A modern mill can produce 500 tonnes of flour a day.

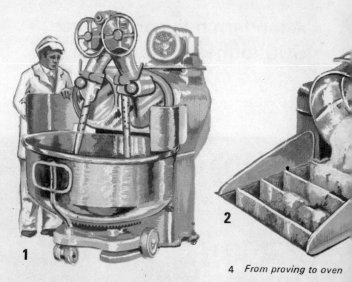

1

2

4 *From proving to oven*

5 *Baked bread coming from oven*

6 *Slicing and wrapping*

A modern bakery

The bakeries of today
also rely on machines
to do most of the work.

From the weighing of the flour
to the slicing of the finished loaf,
the bread is not touched
by human hand.

1 Mixing

2 Mixed dough being
divided

3 Proving the dough

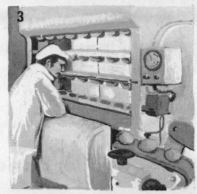

All kinds of bread

Today's bread is very different
from that of olden days.
We have a large choice
when we buy a loaf.

There is white or brown bread,
sliced or unsliced,
and many shapes and sizes
to choose from.

45

Making bread

Ingredients:

      1.2 kg plain flour
      25 g yeast
      750 ml water
      2 teaspoonfuls salt
      25 g butter or margarine

Make sure that all the ingredients are warm.

1 Place the butter
   in a large warm bowl.

2 Sieve the flour and salt
   into the bowl.

3 Put the yeast into a cup
   and stir in a little warm water.

4 Mix until you have
   a white milky fluid.
   Add the yeast mixture
   to the flour and salt.
   Then add the water and mix
   until the dough is soft
   but not sticky.

Making bread (cont'd)

5 Put the dough onto a table top and knead it with your hands until it is thoroughly mixed. This should take about 10 minutes.

6 Put the dough back in the bowl
   and cover with a damp cloth.
   Put the bowl in a warm place
   for about an hour.

7 The dough should have risen
   to about twice its original size.
   Knead the dough
   for another 3 minutes.

8 Shape the dough
   and put it in a baking tin.
   Leave in a warm place
   for about half an hour.

9 Place the tin in an oven
   set at Gas Mark 8 (450°F/230°C).
   Bake for 45 minutes.

10 Take the bread out of the tin
    and allow to cool on a wire tray.

Strange uses of bread

In Russia it is the custom
in restaurants, before eating,
to wipe the cutlery
with a slice of bread.

Crusaders used to place
pieces of mouldy bread
on their wounds.

The mould contained a drug
which helped the wound to heal.

Many centuries later
the drug was rediscovered.

It was called *penicillin.*

Index